SCHOLASTIC

READ & RESPOND

Bringing the best books to life in the classroom

Activities based on **How to Train Your Dragon**
By Cressida Cowell

Recommended system requirements:
Windows: XP (Service Pack 3), Vista (Service Pack 2), Windows 7 or Windows 8 with 2.33GHz processor
Mac: OS 10.6 to 10.8 with Intel Core™ Duo processor
1GB RAM (recommended)
1024 × 768 Screen resolution
CD-ROM drive (24× speed recommended)
Adobe Reader (version 9 recommended for Mac users)
Broadband internet connections (for installation and updates)

For all technical support queries (including no CD drive), please phone Scholastic Customer Services on 0845 6039091.

Designed using Adobe Indesign
Scholastic Education, an imprint of Scholastic Ltd
Book End, Range Road, Witney, Oxfordshire, OX29 0YD
Registered office: Westfield Road, Southam,
Warwickshire CV47 0RA

Printed and bound by Ashford Colour Press
© 2017 Scholastic Ltd
1 2 3 4 5 6 7 8 9   7 8 9 0 1 2 3 4 5 6

British Library Cataloguing-in-Publication Data
A catalogue record for this book is available from the British Library.
ISBN 978-1407-16067-2

Due to the nature of the web, we cannot guarantee the content or links of any site mentioned. We strongly recommend that teachers check websites before using them in the classroom.

Author Sally Burt and Debbie Ridgard
Editorial team Rachel Morgan, Jenny Wilcox, Rebecca Rothwell, Jennie Clifford
Series designer Neil Salt
Designer Anna Oliwa
Illustrator Gemma Hastilow
Digital development Hannah Barnett, Phil Crothers and MWA Technologies Private Ltd

Acknowledgements
The publishers gratefully acknowledge permission to reproduce the following copyright material:
Hachette Children's Books for the use of text extracts and the cover from *How to Train Your Dragon* by Cressida Cowell, first published in the UK by Hodder Children's, an imprint of Hachette Children's Books, 338 Euston Road, London, NW1 3BH. Text and illustrations © 2003, Cressida Cowell (2003, Hodder Children's Books).

Every effort has been made to trace copyright holders for the works reproduced in this book, and the publishers apologise for any inadvertent omissions.

CONTENTS ▼

INTRODUCTION

Read & Respond provides teaching ideas related to a specific children's book. The series focuses on best-loved books and brings you ways to use them to engage your class and enthuse them about reading.

The book is divided into different sections.

- **About the book and author:** gives you some background information about the book and the author.

- **Guided reading:** breaks the book down into sections and gives notes for using it with guided reading groups. A bookmark has been provided on page 12 containing comprehension questions. The children can be directed to refer to these as they read.

- **Shared reading:** provides extracts from the children's book with associated notes for focused work. There is also one non-fiction extract that relates to the children's book.

- **Grammar, punctuation & spelling:** provides word-level work related to the children's book so you can teach grammar, punctuation and spelling in context.

- **Plot, character & setting:** contains activity ideas focused on the plot, characters and the setting of the story.

- **Talk about it:** has speaking and listening activities related to the children's book. These activities may be based directly on the children's book or be broadly based on the themes and concepts of the story.

- **Get writing:** provides writing activities related to the children's book. These activities may be based directly on the children's book or be broadly based on the themes and concepts of the story.

- **Assessment:** contains short activities that will help you assess whether the children have understood the concepts and curriculum objectives. They are designed to be informal activities to feed into your planning.

The activities follow the same format:

- **Objective:** the objective for the lesson. It will be based upon a curriculum objective, but will often be more specific to the focus being covered.

- **What you need:** a list of resources you need to teach the lesson, including digital resources (printable pages, interactive activities and media resources, see page 5).

- **What to do:** the activity notes.

- **Differentiation:** this is provided where specific and useful differentiation advice can be given to support and/or extend the learning in the activity. Differentiation by providing additional adult support has not been included as this will be at a teacher's discretion based upon specific children's needs and ability, as well as the availability of support.

The activities are numbered for reference within each section and should move through the text sequentially – so you can use the lesson while you are reading the book. Once you have read the book, most of the activities can be used in any order you wish.

Below are brief guidance notes for using the CD-ROM. For more detailed information, please click on the '?' button in the top right-hand corner of the screen.

The program contains:

- the extract pages from the book
- all of the photocopiable pages from the book
- additional printable pages
- interactive on-screen activities
- media resources.

Getting started

Put the CD-ROM into your CD-ROM drive. If you do not have a CD-ROM drive, phone Scholastic Customer Services on 0845 6039091.

- For Windows users, the install wizard should autorun. If it fails to do so, then navigate to your CD-ROM drive. Then follow the installation process.
- For Mac users, copy the disk image file to your hard drive. After it has finished copying, double-click it to mount the disk image. Navigate to the mounted disk image and run the installer. After installation the disk image can be unmounted and the DMG can be deleted from the hard drive.
- To install on a network, see the ReadMe file located on the CD-ROM (navigate to your drive).

To complete the installation of the program, you need to open the program and click 'Update' in the pop-up. Please note – this CD-ROM is web-enabled and the content will be downloaded from the internet to your hard drive to populate the CD-ROM with the relevant resources. This only needs to be done on first use; after this you will be able to use the CD-ROM without an internet connection. If at any point any content is updated, you will receive another pop-up upon start up when there is an internet connection.

Main menu

The Main menu is the first screen that appears. Here you can access: terms and conditions, registration links, how to use the CD-ROM, and credits. To access a specific book, click on the relevant button. (Note only titles installed will be available.) You can filter by the

drop-down lists if you wish. You can search all resources by clicking 'Search' in the bottom left-hand corner. You can also log in and access favourites that you have bookmarked.

Resources

By clicking on a book on the Main menu, you are taken to the resources for that title. The resources are: Media, Interactives, Extracts, and Printables. Select the category and then launch a resource by clicking the 'Play' button.

Teacher settings

In the top right-hand corner of the screen is a small 'T' icon. This is the teacher settings area. It is password protected, and the password is: login. This area will allow you to choose the print quality settings for interactive activities ('Default' or 'Best') and also allow you to check for updates to the program or re-download all content to the disk via 'Refresh all content'. You can also set up user logins so that you can save and access favourites. Once a user is set up, they can enter by clicking the login link underneath the 'T' and '?' buttons.

Search

You can access an all-resources search by clicking the 'Search' button on the bottom left of the Main menu. You can search for activities by type (using the drop-down filter) or by keyword by typing into the box. You can then assign resources to your favourites area or launch them directly from the search area.

CURRICULUM LINKS

Section	Activity	Curriculum objectives
Guided reading		Comprehension: To develop positive attitudes to reading and understanding of what they read.
Shared reading	1	Comprehension: To check that the text makes sense to them, discussing their understanding and explaining the meaning of words in context.
	2	Comprehension: To draw inferences such as inferring characters' feelings, thoughts and motives from their actions, and justifying inferences with evidence.
	3	Comprehension: To discuss words and phrases that capture the reader's interest and imagination.
	4	Comprehension: To identify how language, structure and presentation contribute to meaning.
Grammar, punctuation & spelling	1	Composition: To use the forms 'a' or 'an' according to whether the next word begins with a consonant or a vowel.
	2	Composition: To form nouns using a range of prefixes.
	3	Transcription: To use capital letters.
	4	Transcription: To place the possessive apostrophe accurately in words with regular plurals.
	5	Composition: To extend the range of sentences with more than one clause by using a wider range of conjunctions including 'when', 'if', 'because', and 'although'.
	6	Composition: Using conjunctions, adverbs and prepositions to express time and cause.
Plot, character & setting	1	Comprehension: To discuss words and phrases that capture the reader's interest and imagination.
	2	Comprehension: To identify themes and conventions in a wide range of books.
	3	Composition: To organise paragraphs around a theme.
	4	Comprehension: To identify main ideas drawn from more than one paragraph and summarise these.
	5	Spoken language: To participate in discussions, presentations, performances, role play, improvisations and debates.
	6	Spoken language: To ask relevant questions to extend their understanding and knowledge.
	7	Comprehension: To infer characters' feelings, thoughts and motives from their actions, and justify inferences with evidence.
	8	Comprehension: To predict what might happen from details stated and implied.

Section	Activity	Curriculum objectives
Talk about it	1	Spoken language: To participate in discussions, presentations, performances, role play, improvisations and debates.
	2	Spoken language: To participate in discussions, presentations, performances, role play, improvisations and debates.
	3	Spoken language: To consider and evaluate different viewpoints, attending to and building on the contributions of others.
	4	Spoken language: To participate in discussions, presentations, performances, role play, improvisations and debates.
	5	Spoken language: To gain, maintain and monitor the interest of the listeners.
	6	Spoken language: To use spoken language to develop understanding through speculating, hypothesising, imagining and exploring ideas.
Get writing	1	Composition: To plan their writing by discussing writing similar to that which they are planning to write in order to understand and learn from its structure, vocabulary and grammar.
	2	Composition: To use simple organisational devices in non-narrative texts.
	3	Comprehension: To retrieve and record information from non-fiction.
	4	Composition: To use and punctuate direct speech.
	5	Composition: To proofread for spelling and punctuation errors; to read aloud their own writing to a group or the whole class, using appropriate intonation and controlling the tone and volume so that the meaning is clear.
	6	Composition: To assess the effectiveness of their own and others' writing and suggesting improvements.
Assessment	1	Spoken language: To give well-structured descriptions, explanations and narratives for different purposes, including for expressing feelings.
	2	Comprehension: To understand what they read.
	3	Composition: To draft and write.
	4	Comprehension: To check that the text makes sense to them, discuss their understanding and explain the meaning of words in context.
	5	Composition: To create settings, characters and plot in narratives.
	6	Transcription: To write from memory simple sentences dictated by the teacher that include words and punctuation taught so far.

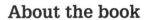

HOW TO TRAIN YOUR DRAGON

About the book

This is the first of a twelve-part (and hopefully more) fantasy adventure series for children set in the Viking age.

The story revolves around a likeable but most unlikely character, Hiccup Horrendous Haddock the Third, son of Stoick the Vast, a Viking chief, and Hope and Heir to the Tribe of the Hairy Hooligans. Hiccup and nine other Viking boys have to prove their worth to be accepted into the Tribe. Their adventures take place on the Island of Berk, where Hiccup befriends an obstinate but lovable dragon and learns to become a Hero the Hard Way.

This is a fast-paced story, loaded with humour, drama, horror, heroics and page-turning cliff-hangers. Cressida Cowell engages her readers with her unique style. The pages are enticingly dotted with childlike scribbles, sketches, maps and ink blots to create an entertaining read.

In 2010, the first book was made into a 3D computer-animated film by DreamWorks Animation. The film earned nominations for the Oscars and BAFTA and it won ten Annie awards. In 2014, Dreamworks Animation released a sequel and another film is due for release in 2018.

About the author

Cressida Cowell is an English children's author, best known for her novel series *How to Train Your Dragon*. She was born in 1966 in London, where she also grew up. She enjoyed many holidays on a small, uninhabited island off the west coast of Scotland where her parents built a stone cottage. The island had no roads or shops and, as they had no telephone or television, Cowell spent many hours drawing, writing, fishing and searching for dragons. In the evenings, her father told stories about the Vikings who raided the area and legends about the dragons who lived in the surrounding caves. Unsurprisingly, this childhood setting was where the idea for her stories began.

She went on to study English at Oxford University, and illustration and graphic design at St Martin's and Brighton University. She wrote her first book, *Little Bo Peep's Library Book*, in 1999 while still at art school. Her other children's books include the *Emily Brown* series (with Neal Layton) *There's No Such Thing as a Ghostie!*, *Daddy on the Moon* and *Hiccup the Seasick Viking*. She wrote and illustrated the first *How to Train Your Dragon* book in 2003, and continued to both write and illustrate the entire series.

She lives in London with her husband and three children. She enjoys reading books, watching films and plays, the sea, boats, chocolate, drawing and dragons.

Key facts

How to Train Your Dragon

First published: 2003

Author: Cressida Cowell

Illustrator: Cressida Cowell

Awards: Mentioned in the '100 Best Children's Books Ever (Novels)' (*The Daily Telegraph*)

Did you know?: The book has sold over 100,000 copies and is published in 30 languages.

Let's begin

Reflect on the title of the book. Most children will be familiar with the title from the film. Some children may not be aware that the book came first and was later adapted for the screen. Ask: *If you see a film before reading the book, do you expect the characters to be similar in the book? Will the story be exactly the same?* If they have seen the film and read the book, ask which one they preferred. Encourage discussion.

Encourage the children to inspect the cover before opening the book. Book covers may vary slightly so answers may differ. Ask: *What images and text appear on the cover?* (the title and author, a large green dragon and a young Viking, old style font) Read the blurb at the back of the book. Ask: *From the blurb, what and who can the reader expect to find in this story?* (Hiccup – a Viking, a toothless dragon, a gigantic dragon, a fight, jokes, funny drawings, dramatic scenes) *Does it sound like a fun or serious book to read?* (fun)

Direct the children to open the cover and look at the first page (this may not exist in older editions). Read the 'Warning' together. Ask: *What is the message in the warning?* (The story is not factual.) *Is it a serious warning?* (no)

Encourage the children to scan the book for pictures and images. Ask: *What do they notice about them?* (They are funny and childlike, with messy ink blots and scribbled words.)

Meet the Tribe

Go to the pictures of the characters and ask: *What is a novice?* (a beginner) *What do their names suggest?* (Their names describe something about them.) Read 'A Note from Hiccup' and look at the picture. Ask: *What type of character is Hiccup?* (an ordinary boy, not a typical-looking Viking/hero) *According to the note, who is telling the story as it happened?* (Hiccup tells the story looking back on the events.)

The setting

Refer the children to the map in the preliminary pages and question 18 on the bookmark (page 12). Ask: *Why has the author included a map?* (Berk is not a real place so the map helps the reader imagine it and link all the places in the story.) *What do the names of the places on the map suggest?* (They are literal descriptions – 'Unlandable Cove' is a dangerous place to land in your boat.) *Who lives where?* (Work through the map.) *How would you describe this place?* (dangerous, scary, wild) *From the description in the second part of Chapter 3, what can you add to your description of the place?* (wet, marshy, cold, muddy, harsh) Encourage using a thesaurus to find synonyms.

Initiation (Chapters 1–3)

Read the first five paragraphs of Chapter 1. Ask: *What is your first impression of Hiccup and Gobber the Belch* (Hiccup: important but, as his name suggests, sickly, unpopular, hesitant; Gobber: loud, commanding, bossy, in charge.) *What is the purpose of the gathering?* (Ten boys, including Hiccup, must pass the Dragon Initiation Programme to become members of the Tribe.) Continue reading until Gobber says 'FIRST CATCH YOUR DRAGON!'. Ask: *Why must Hiccup lead them?* (He is the chief's son.) *How do the other boys feel about this?* (They think he is useless.) *The boys all seem to be excited about this test. Why isn't Hiccup?* (He knows more about dragons than anyone else and realises going to catch one is madness.) Complete the first chapter. Then ask: *What is Gobber's motto for the Tribe?* ('Only the strong can belong', and later 'DEATH OR GLORY'.)

Read Chapter 2. Focus on the comparison between Snotlout and Hiccup and refer to question 4 on the bookmark. Ask the children to explain why Hiccup doesn't look or seem like a Viking Hero. Encourage discussion. Gobber's plan seemed straightforward. Ask: *What went wrong?* (The dragons woke up and chased after the boys.) Ask: *How would you describe this escape?* (funny) Discuss question 17 on the Guided Reading bookmark. *Who is the hero in this chapter?* (Gobber – he saves the boys from the attacking dragons.)

After reading Chapter 3 together, refer to the title of the chapter. Ask: *What is an exile?* (A person forced to leave his or her country or community.) *Why is this a good title?* (It sums up the two extreme possible outcomes of their attempt to catch dragons.)

The first three chapters are full of action, highs and lows. Discuss Hiccup's rollercoaster emotions from the beginning to the end of this section (He feels anxious then fearful, terrified, proud, positive, disappointed, miserable and finally embarrassed.)

Training up (Chapters 4–10)

Read Chapter 4 aloud. Ask: *What do you notice about the title of this chapter?* (It is the same as the book title.) *What is unusual about the Viking book?* (very few words and pages) *How useful do you think it will be? Why?* (Take predictions.)

Refer to question 3 on the Guided Reading bookmark and discuss the names Snotlout suggests for Hiccup's dragon. Ask: *What is Snotlout's intention?* (To bully, disgrace and belittle Hiccup because he thinks he will be a better leader of the Tribe.) *How does Hiccup feel?* (belittled, embarrassed, forlorn)

Refer to question 12 on the bookmark and discuss how capital letters and other punctuation affects the reading aloud.

Read Chapter 5. Ask: *How is Hiccup feeling?* (Incapable/useless at being a hero and doing things the Viking way.) *What advice does Old Wrinkly have for Hiccup?* (To learn to be a Hero the Hard Way, and find alternative dragon training schemes to add to Professor Yobbish's book.)

Read Chapter 6. Explain that this chapter foreshadows what is to come. Ask: *What does this mean?* (There are clues to possible future events in the story.)

As you continue to read Chapters 7, 8 and 9, ask the children to list Hiccup's challenges while trying to train Toothless. Have a discussion and share their findings.

Read Chapter 10. Ask: *How would you describe the outcome of the events in this chapter?* (unexpected, disastrous, serious consequences) *How does the tone change?* (from hilarious to serious)

Brains or brawn (Chapters 11–17)

Read Chapter 11 aloud. Refer to question 6 on the Guided Reading bookmark and identify the antagonist that appears in this chapter. Ask: *What tactics do they use to scare the dragon?* (The Tribes create one big yell.) *Describe the dragon's reaction and its attitude towards the Tribe.* (It replies with a larger yell, nonchalantly flicks Gobber away and teasingly blows a kiss.) By the end of the chapter, the Vikings realise their standard method of yelling will not work. Ask: *To whom do they turn?* (Hiccup) *Why is Stoick embarrassed?* (He did not know Hiccup, his own son, could speak Dragonese; he had just banished Hiccup but now he needs him.)

Read to the end of Chapter 15 with the class. Refer to question 9 on the bookmark and ask the children to identify the cliffhangers in each chapter. Ask: *Who is responsible for the plan to slay the dragons?* (Hiccup.) *What is the boys' reaction to the plan?* (They support Hiccup.) *Where is Toothless?* (Toothless only wants to watch.)

Read the title of Chapter 16. Ask: *What does 'fiendish' mean?* (wicked, cruel, evil) *From the title, can they predict what will happen?* Encourage answers. Explain the humour in the title. (Fiendish plans generally don't 'go wrong' because they are so fiendish!)

Complete Chapters 16 and 17 together. Both chapters end with a cliffhanger. At the end of Chapter 17, ask: *Who wants to find out what happens next? Can anyone predict what will happen?*

Unlikely heroes (Chapters 18–19)

Read the title of Chapter 18. Share predictions and ideas of what happens. Point out that this is the turning point in the story: it was a moment that changed the whole worldview of the Hooligan Tribe. Ask: *What do you think prompted Toothless to help Hiccup?* Encourage answers about Hiccup's kindness and offer of friendship finally paying off. *What were the other dragons doing?* (deserting) Read Chapter 18 together and discuss the roles of Hiccup and Toothless in defeating the dragon. *What role did Stoick play in saving Hiccup's life?* (He used his strength, skill and his shield to protect Hiccup from a flying dragon tooth proving that brawn and brains can go well together!) *How did Hiccup know for sure that the dragon was dead?* (He could hear the supper singing.)

Complete the final chapter together. Discuss the emotions that each character felt at different moments in this chapter. Encourage discussion. Ask: *What is important about Stoick's final speech?* (He gives Hiccup a new name – Hiccup the Useful.)

Epilogue

Refer to question 19 on the bookmark. Ask: *Do all stories have an epilogue?* (no) Discuss the general purpose of an epilogue. (It is used as an ending, to tie up loose ends.) *What clues in the epilogue tell us that this story might continue?* Encourage discussion.

Subsequent readings

Re-read the novel to explore different aspects and key features in more depth. Use the questions on the Guided Reading bookmark to focus discussions.

Structure

Divide the book into sections to reflect the plot structure.

- Beginning: Chapters 1–3 First challenge – Catch a dragon

- Build up: Chapters 4–10 Second challenge – Train a dragon

- Climax and resolution: Chapters 11–18 Third challenge – Fight a dragon

Refer to question 8 on the Guided Reading bookmark. Discuss the many other challenges Hiccup faces in the story.

Discuss key chapters in the book that foreshadow events (Chapter 6), introduce a challenge (Chapter 11), act as the climax (Chapter 16) or are pivotal (Chapter 18).

Style

Refer to question 16 on the bookmark. Ask: *Who tells the story?* (Hiccup tells it, but in third person.) Refer to questions 17 and 18 on the bookmark. As you read, encourage the children to notice how the illustrations support the humour in the story. Discuss other techniques the author uses to create a childlike memoire (inkblots, made-up words, scratched-out notes, spelling errors, maps).

Themes

Especially during the re-reading phase, help the children to identify the various themes in the story: friendship, overcoming challenges (personal and physical), leadership styles, rejection versus acceptance, commitment and loyalty, survival. Think of proverbs, sayings or common expressions that summarise some of these themes: never judge a book by its cover; the pen is mightier than the sword; birds of a feather flock together; in for a penny, in for a pound; he who laughs last, laughs longest.

SCHOLASTIC
READ&RESPOND
Bringing the best books to life in the classroom

How to Train Your Dragon
by Cressida Cowell

Focus on...
Meaning

1. What genre is this book?

2. Explain the meaning of the word 'memoir'.

3. The author uses Viking names for all the characters. Explain the meaning of these names.

4. Why is Hiccup not a 'typical' Viking hero? Give examples from the story.

5. How does Hiccup become a hero in the end?

Focus on...
Organisation

6. Who is the main antagonist in the story? Are there others?

7. Who are Hiccup's faithful friends in the story?

8. Name the challenges Hiccup has to overcome.

9. How does the author build tension and anticipation in the book, particularly in the final chapters?

10. What themes run through the story?

SCHOLASTIC
READ&RESPOND
Bringing the best books to life in the classroom

How to Train Your Dragon
by Cressida Cowell

Focus on...
Language and features

11. Is the story told in the present or past tense?

12. How does the author use capitals and exclamations effectively? Give examples.

13. Find synonyms in the story for 'large'.

14. Identify the made-up words in the story.

15. Find examples of first-, second- and third-person narrative.

Focus on...
Purpose, viewpoints and effects

16. The story is narrated from whose viewpoint?

17. How does the author use humour in the story?

18. How do the illustrations add to the story?

19. What is the purpose of the epilogue?

20. Do you think the author intended the story to hold a message for children?

Extract 1

- Read an enlarged copy of the extract with the children following. Get the children to highlight all the speech marks. Ask: *Who is doing all the talking?* (Gobber) *Who is listening?* (Hiccup and the other boys) *Why are Hiccup's words written in italics and without speech marks?* (The words are his thoughts.) Ask: *What is it called when just one person speaks?* (a monologue)

- Refer to question 12 on the Guided Reading bookmark. Encourage the children to look at the use of capital letters in this extract. Ask: *What is the purpose of the capitals?* (to begin sentences, to mark proper nouns, to stress words for effect) Give the children an opportunity to work in pairs to read the extract aloud to each other. Encourage them to focus on how these stressed words affect the way they read.

- Ask: *What is Gobber telling the boys?* (He is giving them instructions.) Ask the children to identify and underline the instructions, then summarise them in a few short steps. They should also think of their own title for the instructions. They can do this verbally or write them down.

- Say: *Identify the informal speech patterns.*
  - colloquial language: 'there'd', 'fatso', 'idiotically stupid'
  - exaggerated punctuation: words in capital letters, ???
  - use of figurative language: 'they will set upon you like piranhas', 'run like thunder', 'stop them in their tracks'
  - use of sarcasm: 'that's reassuring'
  - tone: Gobber laughs at his own jokes while Hiccup mutters disrespectfully to himself
  - onomatopoeia: 'HA HA HA HA!'

Extract 2

- Prepare to read the extract in pairs: decide who will be Old Wrinkly and Hiccup. Since there is so little narration, it can be left out when reading aloud. Allow time for the pairs to prepare their parts, using their extracts to show where to add expression and emotion. Read the extract aloud.

- Discuss the characters' emotions in the dialogue. Infer how they are feeling. Encourage discussion. Circle words used for 'said' that show emotion ('said Hiccup gloomily', 'fumed Old Wrinkly', 'asked Hiccup', 'continued Old Wrinkly', 'said Hiccup crossly') Ask: *Based on this discussion, how would you describe their relationship?* (They are open and honest, they are comfortable and familiar with each other, they respect each other.)

- Consider the structure of the dialogue. Focus on punctuation and spacing. Ask: *What punctuation indicates direct speech?* (inverted commas) Ask the children to underline the words in inverted commas. Ask: *What separates each speaker in the extract?* (a new line)

- Ask: *Is this dialogue formal or informal?* (informal) *Give examples to support your answer.* Discuss examples of each.
  - contractions: 'don't', 'can't', 'they've';
  - colloquialism: 'OK', 'a big lump', 'Who cares?' 'super-small'
  - onomatopoeia: 'oh pshaw'
  - punctuation: 'IMAGINATION', 'Hero the Hard Way', 'LOT'

- Discuss the purpose of this dialogue. Ask: *Based on what you know about the story, why is this dialogue important?* (Hiccup reveals how he feels about himself and what the others think of him. Old Wrinkly foretells that the Tribe needs new leadership and that Hiccup has what it takes. *This* prediction turns out to be correct.)

Extract 3

- Skim the text together. Ask: *Is it a dialogue or a monologue, as in the first two extracts?* (neither) *What type of text is it?* (descriptive paragraph, foreshadowing future events) Read the text aloud and ask the children to find words and phrases in the text that grab their attention. Afterwards, talk about anything they enjoyed about the extract.

- Discuss unusual words and their meanings. Ask: *What is Valhalla?* (Norse mythology: the hall where Odin receives the souls of heroes slain in battle.) Ask the children to highlight descriptive verbs and adjectives on their copy of the text using colour ('raged', 'hurled', 'shrieked', 'averagely enormous', 'largish', 'gobsmackingly vast'). Use a thesaurus to find alternatives to 'big'. Ask: *Do all these words appear in the thesaurus? Why not?* (The author made up some words.)

- Direct the children to underline interesting phrases, expressions and comparisons. Say: *Identify any similes and metaphors in the extract.* ('the wind hurled about the walls like fifty dragons trying to get in', 'like a couple of sleeping babies', 'like wild Viking ghosts having a loud party in Valhalla', 'a great, glistening, evil mountain') *What other comparisons make the dragons sound large?* ('about the size of a largish cliff', 'about twenty times as large as a Tyrannosaurus Rex'.) *Which phrase implies the dragons were dressed for battle?* ('He looked like he was wearing a kind of jewelled armour') *Which phrase shows the dragons were well camouflaged?* ('it was the colour of the ocean itself'). *Which expression implies the second dragon was scarier than the first?* ('enough to give your nightmares nightmares')

Extract 4

- Give four volunteers a chance to read a paragraph of the text. Ask: *What type of text is it and how can you tell?* (A non-fiction text. It provides facts about the topic, is set out in four clear paragraphs, and uses formal and factual language.) *Can you identify the facts?* Ask the children to re-read the text, but this time in a different order – to mix up the paragraphs. Ask: *How important is the order of the information?* (The order can be changed: it does not affect the meaning of the text.) Ask them to suggest where the information comes from and discuss their ideas. (An information text for children in a children's encyclopedia or website about animals or reptiles.)

- Ask the children to underline the headings in the text. Then ask them to go through the text in pairs, underlining the keywords. Remind them that keywords are the important nouns, verbs and adjectives. On the board, draw a basic mind map to show how the text can be summarised. The topic should appear in the middle with the four sub-topics extending out. Ask the children to call out keywords and say where they belong, for example 'eats meat' belongs to the heading 'Hunting'. The order of the keywords is unimportant. They can use their own keywords.

- Focus on each paragraph's main idea. If they were to write a question that each paragraph answers, what would that question be? (How were they discovered? How do they eat? What species of animal are they? Where do they live?) Ask the children to identify other headings they would like to see in order to find out more about the topic.

Extract 1

Chapter 1

Gobber laughed heartily at his little joke, then continued. 'Dragons this size are normally fairly harmless to man, but in these numbers they will set upon you like piranhas. There'd be nothing left of even a fatso like you, Wartihog – just a pile of bones and your helmet. HA HA HA HA! So… you will walk QUIETLY through the cave and each boy will steal ONE sleeping dragon. Lift the dragon GENTLY from the rock and place it in your basket. Any questions so far?'

Nobody had any questions.

'In the unlikely event that you DO wake the dragons – and you would have to be IDIOTICALLY STUPID to do so – run like thunder for the entrance to the cave. Dragons do not like cold weather and the snow will probably stop them in their tracks.'

Probably? thought Hiccup. *Oh, well*, that's *reassuring*.

'I suggest that you spend a little time choosing your dragon. It is important to get one the correct size. This will be the dragon that hunts fish for you, and pulls down deer for you. You will catch the dragon that will carry you into battle later on, when you are much older and a Warrior of the Tribe. But, nonetheless, you want an impressive animal, so a rough guide would be, choose the biggest creature that will fit into your basket. Don't linger for TOO long in there – '

Linger??? thought Hiccup. *In a cave full of three thousand sleeping DRAGONS?*

'I need not tell you,' Gobber continued cheerfully, 'that if you return to this spot *without* a dragon, it is hardly worth coming back at all. Anybody who FAILS this task will be put into immediate exile. The Hairy Hooligan Tribe has no use for FAILURES. Only the strong can belong.'

Extract 2

Chapter 5

'The point is, I just don't see how I am ever going to become a Hero,' said Hiccup gloomily. 'I am the least Heroic boy in the whole Hooligan Tribe.'

'Oh pshaw, this ridiculous Tribe,' fumed Old Wrinkly. 'OK so you are not what we call a born Hero. You're not big and tough and charismatic like Snotlout. But you're just going to have to work at it. You're going to have to learn how to be a Hero the Hard Way.'

'Anyway,' said Old Wrinkly, 'it might be just what this Tribe needs, a change in leadership style. Because the thing is, times are changing. We can't get away with being bigger and more violent than everybody else any more. IMAGINATION. That's what they need and what you've got. A Hero of the Future is going to have to be clever and cunning, not just a big lump with overdeveloped muscles. He's going to have to stop everyone quarrelling among themselves and get them to face the enemy together.'

'How am I going to persuade anybody to do anything?' asked Hiccup. 'They've started calling me HICCUP THE USELESS. That is not a great name for a Military Leader.'

'You have to see the bigger picture, Hiccup,' continued Old Wrinkly, ignoring him. 'You're called a few names. You're not a natural at Bashyball. Who cares? These are very little problems in the grand scheme of things.'

'It's all very well for you to say they are little problems,' said Hiccup crossly, 'but I have a LOT of little problems. I have to train this super-small dragon in time for Thor'sday Thursday or be thrown out of the Hairy Hooligan Tribe for ever.'

Extract 3

Chapter 11

The storm raged through the whole of that night. Hiccup lay unable to sleep as the wind hurled about the walls like fifty dragons trying to get in.

'Let us in, let us in,' shrieked the wind. 'We're very, very hungry.'

Out in the blackness and way out to sea the storm was so wild and the waves so gigantic that they disturbed the sleep of a couple of very ancient Sea Dragons indeed.

The first Dragon was averagely enormous, about the size of a largish cliff.

The second Dragon was gobsmackingly vast. He was the Monster mentioned earlier in this story, the great Beast who had been sleeping off his Roman picnic for the past six centuries or so, the one who had recently been drifting into a lighter sleep.

The great storm lifted both Dragons gently from the seabed like a couple of sleeping babies, and washed them on the swell of one indescribably enormous wave on to The Long Beach, outside Hiccup's village.

And there they stayed, sleeping peacefully, while the wind shrieked horribly all around them like wild Viking ghosts having a loud party in Valhalla, until the storm blew itself out and the sun came up on a beach full of Dragon and very little else.

***

The first Dragon was enough to give you nightmares.

The second Dragon was enough to give your nightmares nightmares.

Imagine an animal about twenty times as large as a Tyrannosaurus Rex. More like a mountain than a living creature – a great, glistening, evil mountain. He was so encrusted with barnacles he looked like he was wearing a kind of jewelled armour but, where the little crustaceans and the coral couldn't get a grip, in the joints and crannies of him, you could see his true colour. A glorious, dark green, it was the colour of the ocean itself.

Extract 4

The Komodo dragon

Discovery

In 1912, Western scientists discovered a large, dragon-like creature living on the island of Komodo in Indonesia. This man-eating beast went by the local name 'ora, buaya darat', meaning land crocodile. For over a hundred years, scientists have studied this fearsome animal.

Hunting

Komodo dragons are carnivores and fierce hunters. In their natural habitat, they are at the top of the food chain, eating large prey including pigs, deer and even water buffaloes, as well as snakes and fish. They have sharp vision and an acute sense of smell to hunt prey. Although they are quick on their feet, they prefer to hunt by stealth, sometimes waiting hours for their prey to come along to be ambushed. They spring up, knock the prey over and then, with their large claws and about 60 short, sharp teeth, they bite, and eat their prey.

Species

The Komodo dragon is a lizard – the largest, heaviest lizard on Earth. It is a large reptile found in Africa and across Asia. They have a giant, thick tail as long as the body and can grow up to three metres in length – weighing up to 70kg in total. They have short legs, a flat head and a long, forked, yellow tongue used to smell and taste. Their skin is tough and scaly, covered with bony plates. They are well camouflaged and protected by this speckled, brownish yellow, green or grey skin.

Habitat

Komodos live in hot, dry grasslands or forests near rivers or the beach. With their strong forelegs, they dig burrows in which they sleep and lay large eggs. Komodo dragon mothers incubate the eggs (called a clutch) for about three months. Once hatched, the baby dragons run away and climb trees to escape being eaten by the mother or other dragons. After four years, they come down from the trees and live on the ground. Those that survive can live up to 30 years.

GRAMMAR, PUNCTUATION & SPELLING

1. An article – a particle

Objective

To use 'a' or 'an'.

What you need

Photocopiable page 22 'a or an', interactive activity 'a or an'.

What to do

- Say or sing the alphabet; children must clap to replace all the vowels. Repeat, clapping the consonants and sounding the vowels. Using the children's names, identify which ones begin with a vowel or a vowel sound, for example, Alice, Ethan, Isla, Oliver, Uma, Yvette.

- Write these examples on the board: a dragon; an enormous dragon; an honest dragon; a hairy dragon. Ask a volunteer to make up a rule to explain when to use 'a' and 'an'. Explain it does not depend on how you write the word, but how you say the word ('a' + consonant sound, 'an' + vowel sound). If an adjective appears before the noun, 'a' or 'an' must agree with the initial sound of the adjective.

- The words 'a' and 'an' are determiners known as indefinite articles that are used before singular, countable nouns. 'A' and 'an' refers to one so you cannot use 'a' or 'an' with plural nouns or non-countable nouns (like air, fun, advice, information). Go through photocopiable page 22 'a or an' to consolidate the children's understanding.

- Arrange the children in pairs. Show a word and let them make a short sentence using the correct article: eerie – I heard an eerie sound; hour – It took an hour to cook supper; dragon – There is a hairy dragon in my backyard.

Differentiation

Extension: Complete the interactive activity 'a or an' to reinforce this session and discover tricky words that begin with a consonant but have a vowel sound.

2. Fixed on prefixes

Objective

To form nouns using prefixes.

What you need

Printable page 'Cut outs for prefixes', dictionaries, interactive activity 'Puzzling prefixes'.

What to do

- Write these words on the board: angle, disappear, unknown, happy. Ask: *Which are root words only?* (angle, happy) *Which words contain a prefix plus a root word?* (disappear, unknown)

- Revise prefixes by asking volunteers to give an explanation. (A prefix is a group of letters added to the beginning of a word. The spelling of the root word usually stays the same.)

- Consider how prefixes change the meaning of the root words. Display some examples: unhappy; triangle; recharge. Say: *Identify the prefix and then explain how it changes the meaning of the word.* (un = not, tri = three, re = do it again) Ask: *Which part of speech are each of these words?* (triangle – noun; unhappy – adjective; recharge – verb) Discuss how the class of the word with a prefix remains the same as the original root word.

- Arrange the children into small groups. Hand each group a set of cut outs from printable page 'Cut outs for prefixes'. They must use all the cut outs to join root words and prefixes. Then, ask them to arrange the words into word classes to show nouns, verbs and adjectives. Let them use the words in a sentence to demonstrate meaning and function.

- Children complete the interactive activity 'Puzzling prefixes' using prefixes to form nouns, verbs and adjectives.

Differentiation

Support: Let the children use dictionaries and work in pairs.
Extension: Write sentences using words from the cut outs on printable page 'Cut outs for prefixes'.

3. Using CAPITALS

Objective

To use capital letters.

What you need

Copies of *How to Train Your Dragon*, printable page 'Discuss CAPITALS', paper.

What to do

- Ask the children to name punctuation rules for using capital letters. (To start a sentence, begin direct speech, for names, titles and places.)

- Let them follow as you re-read from Chapter 3, from 'Sometime later, when Gobber reckoned they were a safe distance from Wild Dragon Cliff, he yelled at the boys to stop' until he shouts 'HEROES OR EXILE'. Ask: *How has the author used capital letters in the last part of this extract?* (for expression) In pairs, let them re-read the extract to each other, as if there were no capital letters in the text. Ask: *What effect does this have?* (The text loses meaning and expression.)

- Using printable page 'Discuss CAPITALS', the children work in groups to find examples from Chapter 3 of how capitals are used.

- Groups can sit in a circle and play 'Sentence check'. Hand out slips of paper and instruct the children to each write a short sentence about Gobber and the boys, leaving out the punctuation. Once done, they should pass the slips of paper to their left and then edit the sentence received. Finally, pass the sentence to the left again for the next person to check. Repeat as often as time permits.

Differentiation

Support: Encourage self-editing on written work, giving support where necessary.
Extension: Encourage independent self-editing on all written work.

4. Hero's heroes

Objective

To use plural and possessive 's'.

What you need

Extract 3, interactive activity 'Revise contractions', photocopiable page 23 'Plural or possessive?'.

What to do

- Hand out copies of Extract 3 and ask the children to re-read the extract, highlighting all the plural words (walls, dragons, waves, centuries, babies, ghosts, nightmares, barnacles, crustaceans, joints, crannies). Ask: *How does each word end?* (with 's' or 'ies') Ask them to go through the extract again and find any words showing possession (Hiccup's village). Ask: *How do you know it is possessive?* (something belongs to something, ends with 's')

- On the board write three headings: Plural, Possession, Neither. Display one of the following words and ask a volunteer to decide where to place it. Once all the words are placed, discuss any incorrectly placed words. (Vikings – plural, dragon's – possession, useless – neither, there's – neither, Snotlout's – possession, tribes – plural, it's – neither.)

- Discuss the difference between possessives and contractions, giving examples: there's = there is, it's = it is, he's = he is. (In contractions, apostrophes indicate omitted letters from joined words). Contractions including 'is' ('s) are often confused with the 's used to show possession. Complete the interactive activity 'Revise contractions' to practise.

- Using photocopiable page 23 'Plural or possessive', the children identify the plural and possessive words in context. Then ask them to write a sentence for each word to show they understand the different meanings of the words on the back of the sheet.

Differentiation

Extension: Using the words from the photocopiable sheet, let the children write their own sentences showing the words in context.

5. Extend yourself

Objective

To extend sentences with more than one clause using a wider range of conjunctions.

What you need

Individual whiteboards, interactive activity 'Join up'.

What to do

- Display a sentence on the board: Hiccup felt discouraged. Ask: *Is this a phrase or a clause? How can you tell?* (It is a clause because it contains a verb. It is also a complete sentence. A phrase is not a complete sentence and does not contain a verb.)

- Write another sentence on the board: Toothless deserted him. Ask: *Can you join this sentence to the other using 'when' or 'after'?* Let them discuss the answer in small groups or pairs, using their individual whiteboards to write it down. (For example, 'Hiccup felt discouraged *when* Toothless deserted him.' 'Hiccup felt discouraged *after* Toothless deserted him.') Ask: *What do we call these joining words?* (conjunctions or linking words)

- Write another sentence on the board: Hiccup needed support. Ask: *How can you add this clause to the others using 'because'?* Again, let them discuss in groups, writing their final answer on their whiteboard. ('Hiccup felt discouraged *when/ after* Toothless deserted him *because* he needed support.') Ask: *How could you write this another way using 'so'?* Give them time to discuss and experiment in their groups. ('Toothless deserted Hiccup when Hiccup needed support so he felt discouraged.') Discuss different answers.

- Let them practise building sentences using the interactive activity 'Join up'.

Differentiation

Extension: Find examples from the story where conjunctions join sentences.

6. Position it

Objective

To express time, place and cause using prepositions.

What you need

Balls, hula-hoops or beanbags, photocopiable page 24 'Draw it', interactive activity 'Picture the preposition'.

What to do

- A preposition connects a verb, noun or adjective to a noun or pronoun and is found *before* the noun or pronoun it modifies. For example: He threw the ball *to* me. A preposition can change the meaning of a sentence: He threw the ball *to/with/at/behind/after* me. Ask a volunteer to use actions to demonstrate how the meaning changes.

- Play a game to revise using prepositions. Adjust the game according to the space you have available. The children should move around until you give an instruction. The last person to follow the instruction correctly is 'out'. You could use balls, hula-hoops or beanbags for variety. Use different prepositions to express time, place and cause/manner. Instructions might include: bounce the ball; throw the ball into the hoop; pass the beanbag between your legs to a partner; throw the ball after me; place the beanbag on your head and race against your partner.

- Display the following incomplete sentences: She arrived…an ambulance. The toddler jumped…her arms. My dad sang…the circus. The car drove… them. Think…your decision. In pairs, ask the children to add a preposition to complete each sentence. Afterwards, share and discuss the different answers and their meanings.

- Hand out photocopiable page 24 'Draw it' for the children to complete individually.

Differentiation

Support: Using the interactive activity 'Picture the preposition', the children must visualise the correct preposition.

a or an

- 'a' and 'an' are indefinite articles. Find an example of each one in the first chapter of the story.

    1. _____

    2. _____

- Sort the following dragon names into two categories to show when to use 'a' and when to use 'an'.

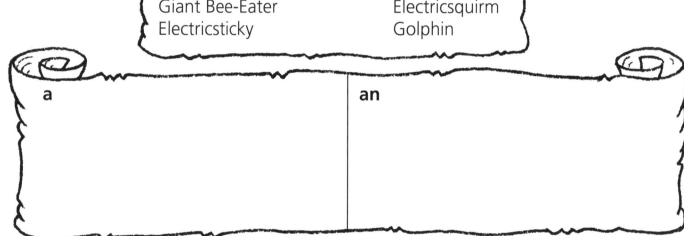

Eight-legged Battlegore   Sharkworm
Hogfly   Itchyworm
Giant Bee-Eater   Electricsquirm
Electricsticky   Golphin

a | **an**

- Fill in 'a' or 'an' in the sentences below.

    1. Hiccup saw _____ whole pile of dragons in the cave.

    2. Hiccup wasn't your usual thug of _____ Hairy Hooligan but he wasn't _____ coward either.

    3. Snotlout was eager to get _____ awesome dragon.

    4. The Gronckle was _____ heavily-armoured brute.

    5. It opened _____ evil, crocodile eye, then closed it.

    6. Hiccup grabbed _____ unconscious-looking dragon.

    7. Fishlegs was keen to find _____ really cool dragon.

    8. Fishlegs sneezed _____ enormous sneeze.

    9. The boys made _____ early dash for the exit.

Plural or possessive?

- In each sentence, underline plural nouns and circle possessive noun forms. Sort the words into the spaces below.

'We need our dragons,' said Hiccup, 'so let's start calling for them.'

Each novice's dragon was not far away.

They were hiding quite close, crouching like cats in Berk's boggy bracken.

The fickle-hearted creatures were planning their next move – to obey or desert their masters.

'We could serve the New Master instead of this bunch of losers,' suggested Seaslug.

'That green Devil's appetite is too big! We might be his next meal!' remarked Horrorcow.

'Let's rather obey until we are sure Stoik's Tribe has lost,' hissed Fireworm.

So, the dragons returned, landing on each boy's outstretched arm.

Hiccup explained the plan to defeat the Tribe's worst nightmare – Seadragonus Giganticus Maximus.

Hiccup's dragon, Toothless, wasn't interested in helping his peers.

Plural nouns	Possessive nouns

Draw it

● Draw a simple diagram to demonstrate the meaning of the prepositions in each sentence.

We flew the kite **into/above/beyond** the tall tree.

I took a picture of the horizon **at/before/after** sunset.

The little boy arrived **with/on/without** his big brother.

We heard the story **about/in/behind** the broken-down bus.

1. All in a name

Objective

To discuss interesting words and phrases.

What you need

Copies of *How to Train Your Dragon*, Photocopiable page 29 'Name it'.

Cross-curricular link

History

What to do

- Ask the children if their name has a meaning or an origin. Encourage discussion. Some names come from certain places, some names are a combination of names, and some names are nicknames. If time permits, research the names of the children in the class.

- Most of the names in the story describe something about the person. Say: *Find examples of names that provide clues about the characters* (for example, Dogsbreath, Speedifist, Clueless). The Vikings used riddle-like phrases called kennings to describe things. A kenning is a descriptive expression, often a hyphenated compound word, used instead of a noun or a name. Brainstorm examples such as: ankle-biter = a young child; tree swinger = monkey; Lord of laughter = Norse god Loki; slayer of giants = Thor; whale road = the ocean; motor mouth = someone who talks a lot; mind reader = someone who knows what you are thinking.

- In small groups, ask the children to find ten names from the story and discuss their associations. Remember to look through the list of dragon names at the end of the book. Discuss the meaning of names like 'Raptortongue' and 'Sabre-Tooth Driver'.

- The children should complete photocopiable page 29 'Name it', matching names to characters.

Differentiation

Extension: Think up a kenning for characters from other stories (Giant-slayer = Jack from 'Jack and the Beanstalk', Cinder-sweeper = Cinderella).

2. Themes are like threads

Objective

To identify themes and conventions.

What you need

Interactive activity 'Identify themes', printable page 'Make a patchwork', different-coloured markers.

What to do

- Ask: *Who has attended a theme party? Can you describe what it is?* (When you have to dress up according to a topic, such as Halloween.)

- In literature, a theme is a main idea or topic that weaves its way through the story. To identify the theme (or themes) ask the question: *What lesson was learned?* A common theme in stories is 'good triumphs over evil', summarised as 'good vs evil'. Ask: *Can you think of others?* (love, acceptance, death) The theme is key to understanding the plot and the message in the story.

- Conduct a short quiz. Write three headings on the board: Character, Event, Theme. Mention story elements and ask volunteers to categorise each one: Sea Dragon (character); catching a dragon (event); friendship (theme); acceptance (theme). To reinforce this, open up the interactive activity and let the children sort out the themes from other story elements.

- Arrange the children into groups. Hand out printable page 'Make a patchwork' and make sure they have markers. They must identify events in the story that link to the different themes and then colour code them. This activity should spark lots of discussion as they try to sort it out. Answers may vary.

Differentiation

Support: Pick one theme and illustrate a scene from the story relating to it.
Extension: Pick a theme and make a timeline of events relating to the theme.

3. Challenge 1, 2, 3

Objective

To organise paragraphs around a theme.

What you need

Copies of *How to Train Your Dragon*, printable page 'Plot the plot'.

What to do

- Ask a volunteer to explain the meaning of a story 'plot'. (It is a term used to describe the main events in a story. The events link together in a sequence that flows from the beginning to the end of the story – a summary of the story's main events.) Refer the children to the chapter titles in the content section of the book. Ask: *What do you notice about the chapter titles?* (They provide a summary of events in sequence – a basic plot).

- In this book, the plot divides into three main events: Hiccup's first, second and third challenges. Ask: *Which are the three main challenges in the plot?* (catching a dragon; training a dragon; fighting a dragon) Write the answers on the board.

- Point out that Hiccup faced other 'minor' challenges. Ask the children to think of some and write them on the whiteboard in a random order. The children can work with a partner to sort the 'minor' challenges under each of the three major challenges using printable page 'Plot the plot'. Afterwards, discuss their ideas.

- The children should use their notes to write three short paragraphs describing the main challenges. These paragraphs should follow the correct plot sequence.

Differentiation

Support: Children can write short paragraphs of three or four sentences.
Extension: Encourage children to extend their paragraphs to include some of the minor challenges as well.

4. No place like home

Objective

To identify main ideas drawn from more than one paragraph.

What you need

Copies of *How to Train Your Dragon*, photocopiable page 30 'Write a travel brochure'.

Cross-curricular link

Geography

What to do

- Ask: *Has anyone visited a very small island? What was it like? What did you do there?* Encourage discussion about islands. Point out that isle sounds like I'll and is often confused with aisle.

- Refer to the map of Berk. Ask: *Why is it called an 'isle'?* (It is small.) Discuss how the names on the map give clues to what the place is like ('Huge Hill' – a very big hill in the middle; 'Unlandable Cove' – clearly not a good place to land; 'Puffin Point' – inhabited by puffins). How would they describe Berk to a stranger? Write ideas on the board.

- Let the children work in pairs to prepare and plan a travel guide to the Isle of Berk. They should scan the book for descriptions of Berk and write keywords under the headings provided on photocopiable page 30 'Write a travel brochure'. They can also use the board notes.

- Explain that they must use all the information to write their own travel guide for display on A4 paper (or design a digital one). Encourage them to include a picture or map of the place, or its inhabitants.

Differentiation

Support: Provide chapters and page numbers to help children find information on Berk.
Extension: Write a travel brochure for the neighbouring Meathead Islands (South Island).

5. Zero to hero

Objective

To participate in discussion.

What you need

Copies of *How to Train Your Dragon,* printable page 'Show how characters grow'.

What to do

- Re-read Chapter 5. Ask: *What is Hiccup's dilemma?* (He feels he can never be a hero. He feels useless and unable to amount to anything.) Ask: *What does Old Wrinkly feel about this?* (He thinks Hiccup stands a chance of being a leader and a hero, but not in the conventional way.) Ask: *What does Old Wrinkly say about the Tribe's need for change*? (The Tribe needs a new kind of leadership – that shouting, yelling and brute force are not the only way to handle things. He sees potential in Hiccup's ability to talk to dragons and use his head to think though situations.)

- Ask: *How does Hiccup feel about his dragon?* (It is tiny and unimpressive – nothing special.) *How does this change?* (Despite his size, Toothless shows impressive bravery and ability.)

- Let the children work in groups. Assign each group a character from the story (Hiccup, Toothless, Stoick, Snotlout, the Sea Dragon). Using printable page 'Show how characters grow' each group should discuss how this character appeared at first and how/why the character changes according to their: self-confidence; physical strength and ability; attitude towards others; leadership skills; hero status.

- Come together and have a class discussion to share ideas. Compare characters to help the children gain further insight into each character.

Differentiation

Support: Monitor group work and assist and provide prompts and ideas where necessary.
Extension: Use the character growth chart to describe characters in other books.

6. Find out more

Objective

To ask relevant questions to extend their knowledge.

What you need

Media resource 'Viking facts', interactive activity 'True or false'.

Cross-curricular link

Geography

What to do

- The book is set in the time of the Vikings. Ask: *Were the Vikings real or imaginary people?* (real) Read the warning at the beginning of the book ('Any relationship to any historical fact whatsoever is entirely coincidental.'). Ask: *Why do you think the author wrote this?* (The book is a fantasy story – not based on fact, but set in the time of the Vikings.) Ask: *Can we learn things from a fantasy book?*

- Ask the children to tell you what they know about the Vikings based on their general knowledge and elements from the book. Write these randomly on the board or flip chart. Use a different colour to identify unclear facts as these can be verified later.

- Read the information on the media resource 'Viking facts'. Explain that the children must use the information to decide which parts in the story are true or false. Refer to the information on the board and make adjustments where necessary. Complete the interactive activity 'True or false' to reinforce these facts.

- The children then work in small groups to create a Viking factfile using information from the sources available. Groups should divide the task into four or five main questions so each child can research an answer. Groups then pool the information and present it.

Differentiation

Support: Provide resources and time in class to complete the task.

PLOT, CHARACTER & SETTING

7. Friend or foe

Objective

To infer character's feelings, thoughts and motives and justify with evidence.

What you need

Printable page 'Character cards', photocopiable page 31 'Explain the action'.

Cross-curricular link

Citizenship

What to do

- Write the following on the board: Actions speak louder than words! Ask: *What does this expression mean?* (How we behave and act reveals our feelings, thoughts and motives.) *If you want to be someone's friend, how do you show your intentions?* Encourage discussion. Ask: *What qualities does a friend display?* (love, trust, understanding, generosity, loyalty, kindness)

- Children work in groups. Hand out cards from printable page 'Character cards'. You can use all or some of the names, or choose any other characters from the story. Place them face down on the table, then each child must have a turn to flip over two cards together and declare 'friend or foe'. They then describe to the group the relationship between the two characters, explaining how they feel and what they say and do to show this. Point out that the relationship may change during the story and they should explain this. Encourage the rest of the group to add their ideas.

- Hand out photocopiable page 31 'Explain the action'. The children can complete the sentences, in pairs or on their own, to explain each character's motives behind their actions.

Differentiation

Support: Monitor group discussion and assist individuals needing support.
Extension: The children choose a character from the story and explain why they would or would not want them as a friend.

8. What happens next?

Objective

To predict what might happen from details stated and implied.

What you need

Copies of *How to Train Your Dragon,* printable page 'Predict what happens', interactive activity 'What happens next?'.

What to do

- In this book, the author uses foreshadowing and cliffhanger endings as literary devices to keep the reader's attention. Ask: *What is foreshadowing?* (When the reader gets an insight into something about to happen or that will happen later in the story.) *Why are cliffhangers often used in adventure stories?* (A cliffhanger keeps the reader's attention. The outcome is unknown, which creates tension and excitement for the reader and an eagerness to continue reading to find out what happens next. Cliffhangers also increase the pace of the plot.)

- Foreshadowing often occurs at the beginning of a story or chapter, while cliffhangers occur at the end of chapters or episodes. With a partner, ask the children to scan the book for examples of each.

- Both devices leave the reader with questions about what happens next. Using printable page 'Predict what happens', the children should make notes of some of the questions a reader might ask. Go through the examples together then let them work in groups. Let the groups share their examples and questions. Discuss the impact each one has on the reader. (For example, excitement, anticipation, eagerness to carry on reading, wanting to know the outcome, looking out for clues, and so on.)

Differentiation

Support: The children can do the interactive activity 'What happens next?' as reinforcement.
Extension: The children write a cliffhanger ending to a story about their day including foreshadowing.

Name it

- Draw a line to match the name to its description.
- From reading the story, add other words describing these characters. You can also use a thesaurus to find synonyms.

Clueless	Ready	_____
Dogsbreath	Stubborn	_____
Speedifist	Smelly	_____
Wartihog	Bungling	_____
Tuffnut	Overweight	_____

- Identify these characters from the book. Explain each name.

Dragon-spotter (Chapter 10) _____

_____

Invincible monster (Chapter 12) _____

_____

Killing-machines (Chapter 13) _____

_____

Terrors of the seas (Chapter 19) _____

_____

- Draw a picture and make up your own Viking name for:

Another Sea Dragon	An enemy Viking chief

Write a travel brochure

● Make notes from the book then write your own paragraphs about this travel destination.

The landscape	The weather
The people	**The animals**
The food	**Entertainment**
Places of interest	**Dangers**

Explain the action

● Complete each sentence to explain the actions of the characters.

1. Toothless bit Hiccup because _____

_____

2. Stoick banished his son because _____

_____

3. Gobber saved the boys from the angry dragons because _____

_____

4. Toothless obeyed Hiccup because _____

_____

5. Snotlout teased Hiccup because _____

_____

6. Hiccup was kind and spoke to Toothless because _____

_____

7. The Green Death wanted to eat both tribes because _____

_____

8. Stoick 'unbanished' Hiccup because _____

_____

9. Toothless saved Hiccup because _____

_____

10. The Hairy Hooligans and the Meatheads came together because _____

_____

TALK ABOUT IT

1. Telling stories

Objective
To tell narratives using expression.

What you need
Copies of *How to Train Your Dragon*, printable page 'Expression checklist', tablets.

Cross-curricular link
Design & technology

What to do

- Re-read Chapter 2. Ask: *Who is telling the story?* (Hiccup) *What narrative voice does he use?* (third-person narrative) *Why?* (Although it is his story, he is the narrator looking back and telling it from the outside.) The author indicates plenty of expression – let the children find examples in the chapter.

- Write the following words of Gobber on the board: 'What in Thor's name happened in the cave?' Say: Imagine if Hiccup were to tell his side of the story, how would the story sound? (It would be in the first person, and would have lots of expression.) In groups, each person retells parts of Hiccup's story. The first person begins with a sentence such as: 'The cavern was full of more dragons than I could ever have imagined existed!' Then the next person makes up a sentence to follow on, for example, 'I was so scared, I was sweating and shaking'. Keep going around the group until the story is complete. Remind them to use as much expression as possible when they tell their parts. Refer to printable page 'Expression checklist' for expression guidelines.

- Encourage the children to find another section of the story to retell in the first person. Let them practise in pairs and then ask volunteers to tell their story to the class.

Differentiation

Support: Record the stories on a tablet and let children review their own and each other's work.

2. Hear all about it

Objective
To participate in role play.

What you need
Extract 2, photocopiable page 35 'Interview a character'.

Cross-curricular links
History, citizenship

What to do

- Ask two volunteers to read the parts of the characters in Extract 2. Ask: *What is the focus of the extract?* (a conversation about Hiccup's problem) Discuss the tone and style of the conversation (informal, personal, expressing feelings, private).

- Compare the elements of a conversation with those of a media interview. Ask: *What is the difference between a conversation and a media interview?* (A media interview is not private and is usually formal, the interviewer asks specific questions to get information from the interviewee.) *Where do interviews usually happen?* (for example, in a studio, on location or at the scene of a crime) *Where do you hear or listen to interviews?* (radio, TV, podcasts, internet, and so on)

- Hand out photocopiable page 35 'Interview a character'. Identify the types of open questions an interviewer might ask (Who? Where? When? What? Why? How?) Explain the difference between open and closed questions.

- Let the children choose an event and character from the book. Ask them to write questions they would like their character to answer about the event.

- Then, in pairs, the children role play the interview using their own questions: one as the character, one as the interviewer, and then they swap around.

Differentiation

Support: Write one question per question type.
Extension: Children can write as many questions per question type as they are able to.

3. Choosing a hero

Objective

To consider and evaluate different viewpoints.

What you need

Extract 2, photocopiable page 36 'Compare viewpoints'.

Cross-curricular link

History

What to do

- Re-read Extract 2 together. Ask: *Does Hiccup think he can be a hero?* (no) *Does Old Wrinkly agree or disagree with Hiccup?* (He agrees that Hiccup is not a born hero, but believes Hiccup can be a future hero.) *Does Hiccup agree or disagree with Old Wrinkly?* (He disagrees – he feels useless.)

- Arrange the children into pairs or small groups and hand out copies of photocopiable page 36 'Compare viewpoints'. Using the photocopiable sheet and Extract 2, the children should list the characteristics of a 'Hero' as viewed by the different characters. They should make notes, adding any other common characteristics, such as 'bravery'. Have a class discussion. Give groups an opportunity to report back briefly and share their views.

- Not everyone in the Hooligan Tribe was ready for a new kind of hero. In their groups, assign a character to each child (Old Wrinkly, Stoik, Snotlout, Mogadon, Professor Yobbish). Have a 'forum discussion' where each child role plays a character's views on the type of hero they believe the Tribe needs, and why. Each character should give reasons for their point of view and examples from the story to support their view (Stoick: I think we need a hero with/that… because…).

Differentiation

Support: Monitor the group discussion. Provide support where necessary.
Extension: Groups can conduct an open discussion in front of the class. The class can then evaluate which characters express their views with clarity.

4. Presenting the Sea Dragon

Objective

To give a presentation.

What you need

Copies of *How to Train Your Dragon*, printable pages 'Dragon card template' and 'Presentation preparation'.

What to do

- Throughout the book, the author includes dragon collector cards. In pairs, ask the children to find them in the book and read them, taking note of the headings and information provided.

- Working with a partner, the children should create a new collector card for the dreaded Sea Dragon. Let them make a template (or use the template on printable page 'Dragon card template') and then find facts from the story found in Chapters 6 and 11–17. Allow time for research.

- Using the information collected, the children should now prepare a presentation. Decide if they will work in pairs or individually. They should use the information on the collector card to guide their presentation but should also be able to expand on the subject. They should include evidence and examples when possible.

- Remind the children that the purpose of a presentation is to relay information to an audience. Discuss how to engage the audience using the presentation tips on printable page 'Presentation preparation'. Explain that confidence comes with good planning, preparation and practice. Provide enough time for this in class.

Differentiation

Support: The children can prepare a presentation based on an existing dragon collector card.
Extension: The children can prepare and present on another creature of their choice – a mythical creature (minotaur), extinct animal (dinosaur) or real-life reptile (iguana). This will require independent research.

▼ TALK ABOUT IT

5. Jokes and riddles

Objective
To gain and maintain the interest of the listener.

What you need
Copies of *How to Train Your Dragon*, media resource 'Jokes and riddling talk'.

Cross-curricular link
Citizenship

What to do

- Focus on Chapter 9. Hiccup tried to motivate Toothless to cooperate with his training in various ways, without success until he tried his final option: jokes and riddling talk. Read the part where Hiccup promises to tell Toothless a joke if he obeys. Ask: *Did Toothless enjoy the joke?* (Yes – he thought it was hysterically funny.) This joke is also a type of riddle. Ask: *What is a riddle? What other jokes are also riddles?* (knock-knock jokes, for example) Open up the media resource 'Jokes and riddling talk' and read the jokes to them. Discuss the humour.

- Have a discussion. Ask: *What makes a joke funny?* (age-appropriateness, an unexpected or obvious punchline, a clever word play, an entertaining style) *When is a joke not funny?* (If it's mean or inappropriate.)

- Explain that they must help Hiccup come up with more jokes and riddles to keep Toothless motivated. In groups, brainstorm jokes (also use joke books or supervised internet research). The jokes should be the type Toothless would enjoy – about fish, Vikings or Sea Dragons! Encourage them to adapt or make up their own jokes.

- Have a joke show where they can present their Toothless jokes to the class in groups or individually.

Differentiation
Extension: Children can research riddles and kennings. They should find examples of each. Based on these examples they can create some of their own.

6. Pros and cons

Objective
To develop understanding through exploring ideas.

What you need
Photocopiable page 37 'Pros and cons'.

Cross-curricular links
History, citizenship

What to do

- Ask: *What do we mean when we talk about the pros and cons of something?* (This means looking at the advantages (pros) and disadvantages (cons) before making a decision. In Latin, *pro* means 'for' and *con* means 'against'.) Discuss a few relevant examples. Ask: *What are the pros and cons of… …moving schools? …going overseas for a holiday? …watching the news on TV every day? …cycling to school? …eating chocolate?* (Various answers encouraging ideas.)

- Arrange the children into small groups. They must discuss, identify and write down scenarios in the story when a decision had to be made (for example, choosing a dragon, following Snotlout or Hiccup as leader of the Tribe, punishing the novices of the Tribe, confronting the Sea Dragon). Encourage them to think of other scenarios – ones not in this story (living on Berk; having a dragon of your own; speaking Dragonese; being a leader or a hero, and so on).

- Hand out photocopiable page 37 'Pros and cons' and in their groups ask them to choose any three topics from the ones discussed. Together, they should consider the pros and cons for each decision and write them down.

- Regroup and have a class discussion to share their thoughts and ideas.

Differentiation
Support: Organise groups carefully or work with selected groups.
Extension: Prepare and present a debate declaring the pros or cons of being a hero today.

Interview a character

- Choose an event and a character from the story.
- Write open questions for this character to answer.
- Role play the character by answering the questions in full.

The event

The character

Who?

Where?

When?

What?

Why?

How?

Compare viewpoints

● Read Chapter 5 then list the qualities of a hero from each point of view.

The Hooligans' idea of a hero

Old Wrinkly's idea of a hero

Hiccup's idea of a hero

Pros and cons

● Choose a topic from the story and list the pros and cons.

Topic _____

Pros

Cons

Topic _____

Pros

Cons

Topic _____

Pros

Cons

▼ GET WRITING

1. Plan a Viking event

Objective
To plan their writing based on other similar texts.

What you need
Copies of *How to Train Your Dragon*, examples of programmes or event posters.

Cross-curricular link
Computing

What to do

- Look at the Thor'sday Thursday programme of events in Chapter 10. Discuss the structure, focusing on the layout and design features (main heading, times and subheadings to show events throughout the day, pictures to add clarity). Identify language features (clear and concise wording, strong vocabulary used to advertise events, 'teasers'). Write these points on the board.

- Ask: *How could this programme be presented or distributed? What is the purpose of this programme? How does the content appeal to a Viking audience? Would this event appeal to a modern audience? What would you change for a similar event today?* Encourage discussion.

- Look at other examples of posters, flyers and notices. Identify the purpose of each one and any similar features (headings, large lettering, a clear message, visual appeal, use of colour or pictures).

- Let the children work together to write a checklist of criteria for things to consider when designing a poster or flyer for an event.

- Using their checklists, children should plan another Viking event and design their own programme as a poster or flyer. Discuss ideas (for example, The Viking Annual Games, The Viking Food Fair, The Best-trained Dragon Competition, The Viking Summer Solstice Festival, The Viking Leadership Training Camp, and so on).

Differentiation
Extension: Make a digital copy of their programme of events.

2. Barbaric book review

Objective
To use simple organisational devices in non-narrative texts.

What you need
Copies of *How to Train Your Dragon*, photocopiable page 41 'Book review collector card'.

What to do

- Refer to 'the book' in Chapter 4, written by Professor Yobbish. Ask: *Does the book have the main features of a published book?* (Yes – it has a front and back cover, a title, an author, a copyright page, the name of the publisher, a dedication, information about the author, a chapter heading, a blurb on the back cover, the price.) Read the blurb on the back of the book. Ask: *Would you have said the same thing about this book?* (open answers) *Is the blurb fact or opinion?* (opinion with some facts)

- Using the template on photocopiable page 41 'Book review collector card', direct the children to work in pairs or small groups to fill in as much information as possible. They should rate aspects of the book and add their own comment/opinion on the back of each card. Give groups an opportunity to share their reviews with the class and discuss any similarities and differences. Ask: *Did everyone give the same ratings?* (no) *Why?* (opinions differ)

- Encourage the children to choose another book to read and review, for example, another book in the series, or other books by the same author. Provide opportunities in class to read the book and complete the book review.

- Display the book reviews around the classroom.

Differentiation
Support: Focus on completing a book review for *How to Train Your Dragon*.
Extension: Children can present their reviews visually and orally to the class.

3. Take note

Objective

To retrieve and record information from non-fiction texts.

What you need

Copies of Extract 4, markers, media resource 'Real reptiles', photocopiable page 42 'Reptile factfile'.

Cross-curricular link

Science

What to do

- Re-read Extract 4. Ask: *What are keywords?* (important nouns, adjectives or verbs highlighting the main idea of a text) *When do we use them?* (to summarise, make notes, study, make lists, advertise)

- Working in pairs, the children should highlight the keywords. Together, go through the text and discuss variations in their word choices.

- Guide the children to rewrite the information in their own words, using their keywords. If time is limited, share the text out among groups.

- Look at pictures of other reptiles from media resource 'Real reptiles' or the internet. Let children choose another reptile to research. Using photocopiable page 42 'Reptile factfile', they should make notes under each heading using keywords. Having made notes, they rewrite the information in their own words. Provide resources and time in class. Display their information sheets on the walls.

- Discuss common characteristics of the reptiles and compare them to the dragons in the story.

Differentiation

Support: Provide source information, help children to make notes and guide the writing process.
Extension: Children can use their note-taking skills to do a research project for a non-fiction booklet or display board called 'Your guide to dragons and other reptiles'.

4. Speaking directly

Objective

To use direct speech.

What you need

Copies of *How to Train Your Dragon*, photocopiable page 43 'Show the inverted commas', interactive activity 'Add inverted commas'.

What to do

- Ask a volunteer to explain the difference between indirect and direct speech, and name the punctuation clues. (Words spoken directly by a character go in inverted commas.)

- Ask the children to scan the book to identify examples of direct speech. Have a class quiz where one child reads a sentence from the story and the others decide if it is direct or indirect speech. (Hiccup let out a yelp – indirect. 'Please stop eating my father's beard,' he yelled – direct.)

- Write this sentence on the board: No! yelled Hiccup, with the best yell he had ever yelled. Ask a volunteer to fill in the inverted commas. Identify the rules (any punctuation used when the character speaks, must be included inside the inverted commas).

- Hand out photocopiable page 43 'Show the inverted commas'. Let them draw a simple cartoon and fill in the speech bubbles. Explain that the speech bubble contains the text, just like speech marks. Complete the rest of the photocopiable sheet.

- Open up the interactive activity 'Add inverted commas' and read the dialogues together. Ask: *What do you notice about the spacing and punctuation?* (A new speaker starts on a new line, missing speech marks.) Let them fill in the missing speech marks, working at their own pace.

- Let them imagine a new scene/conversation from the story and use their skills to write dialogue between two characters.

Differentiation

Support: The children can rewrite an existing dialogue from the story in their own words.

5. Singing supper

Objective

To proofread for spelling and punctuation errors; To read aloud their own writing.

What you need

Media resources 'The Supper Song' and 'What am I?'.

Cross-curricular links

Science, history

What to do

- Open up the media resource 'The Supper Song' and read it aloud. Ask: *Who or what is singing?* (The Green Death/its tooth after it exploded.) *What did the singing mean?* (It is dying/is dead.) *What is it singing about?* (About its life. It is boasting about how great it was. Final/last words.)

- 'Sing out loud until you're eaten' is a key line in the song. Ask: *What does it mean?* (We may as well sing because we will all become supper one day!) Ask: *What specific things does the dragon mention?* (It ruled the ocean and the land and put fear into the wind and the waves.) Look at the tenses used in each verse.

- Open the media resource 'What am I?'. Read each riddle and discuss answers (shark, eagle, lion). Let them choose any animal of prey and write its 'supper song'. Brainstorm things this animal can boast about: physique, abilities, enemies. They can follow the same pattern as the original song: First verse, present tense (I tell… I put… I make…); second verse, past tense (Once I was…. Once I made… I could… I would ….); ending with a riddle – What am I? They must plan, draft and edit their songs.

- Encourage the children to perform their songs using appropriate tone and volume.

Differentiation

Support: The children can write one verse.
Extension: They can write and perform a song about a famous person with the title 'Who am I?'.

6. A letter of complaint

Objective

To assess the effectiveness of their own and others' writing.

What you need

Copies of *How to Train Your Dragon,* media resource 'Letter of complaint'.

Cross-curricular link

Computing

What to do

- Ask: *Who has received a letter? Who has written a letter? Letters used to be the primary form of communication. Why are they hardly used today?* (emails, phones and texting have replaced letter writing) *Why is it still important to know how to write a letter?* (Letters have their own structure and rules. Letter writing is a skill.) *What types of letters are still sent?* (invitations, thank you letters, application letters, letters to editors, lawyers' letters, complaints)

- Read Stoick's letter to Professor Yobbish (Chapter 19). Ask: *What do you notice about the letter? What could be improved?* (messy, incomplete address and date, poor spelling, rude tone, very short, no paragraphs) Revise the elements of letter writing. Open the media resource and read the letter. Ask the children to identify key features (address, title, formal tone, polite, neat, carefully edited). Write these on the board in a random order.

- Discuss ideas, then let the children write a letter of complaint from one character to another (for example, Stoick about banishing the boys, to Snotlout about his attitude towards Hiccup…) The children use the guidelines on the board to edit their work and evaluate their peers' work.

- Type them onto computers and display them.

Differentiation

Support: Rewrite Stoick's letter.
Extension: Write a real letter of complaint about an issue at school or in the community.

Book review collector card

- Review a book using this book review collector card and add it to your collection.

> **Title**

The basic plot

The main characters

> **Interesting facts**

Genre:

Author:

Illustrator:

Number of pages:

Book awards:

> **Rate on a scale 1–5** →

Interest level	Readability	Fun element	Recommend to others
1-2-3-4-5	1-2-3-4-5	1-2-3-4-5	1-2-3-4-5

Reptile factfile

● Use this template to gather and present information on a reptile.

Species
Description
Habitat
Food
Enemies
Picture

Show the inverted commas

- Draw a cartoon of Hiccup and Toothless speaking. Write their words in two speech bubbles.

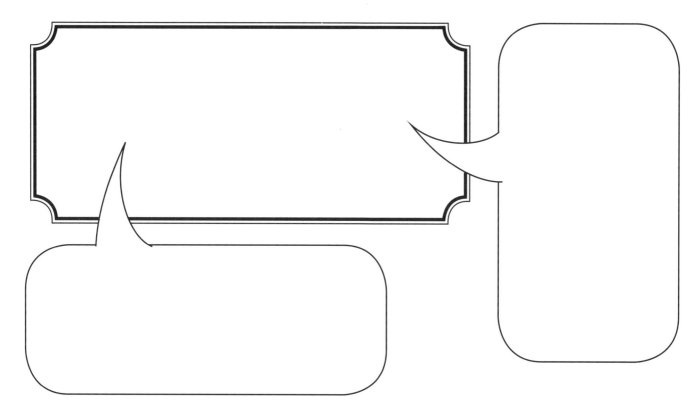

- Fill in the missing inverted commas in each sentence.

1. Fetch! Hiccup commanded and pointed to the sea.

2. Can you speak Dragonese? Stoick enquired sheepishly.

3. Toothless responded, Me want some food now. Me hungry.

4. Everyone yelled, GO AWAY! but the dragon ignored them.

5. You can be a hero of the future, replied Old Wrinkly.

6. You can speak, said Stoick. I've unbanished you.

7. You really do have problems, said Fishlegs amazed.

8. SSSTOPPP!!!!! screamed Gobber and there was an awful silence.

9. Stoick cried N-N-N-OOOOO!!! as Hiccup disappeared.

10. Pardon me… giggled the Dragon evilly. A little party trick…

ASSESSMENT

1. Tell us how

Objective

To give well-structured explanations.

What you need

Copies of *How to Train Your Dragon*, interactive activity 'How to…', printable page 'How to…', printable page 'Presentation preparation'.

Cross-curricular links

Science, computing

What to do

- Refer to the title of the book. Ask: *What type of book does it sound like?* (A manual or textbook.) Ask the children to scan the book for examples of explanations or instructions. (Chapter 1 – how to catch a dragon, Chapter 9 – obedience lessons, Chapter 11 – How to deal with the Sea Dragon, Chapters 14/15 – A new plan of action)

- Discuss important elements of an explanation and write these on the board. (details of who and/ or what is involved; chronological order; clear and concise; the use of adverbials like 'first', 'then', 'finally'; warnings or precautions; end result) Open the interactive activity 'How to…' and let the children complete the activity to reinforce these elements.

- Explain that they should make up their own 'How to…' topic inspired by the story. They will present a well-structured explanation, describing the task in detail. Discuss and share ideas: How to care for a dragon; How to play Bashyball; How to compete at hammer-throwing; How to bury a Viking…

- The children can use printable page 'How to…' to make notes. They should also use the tips for presenting on printable page 'Presentation preparation'. Use this to assess their presentation.

Differentiation

Support: The children can explain 'how to catch a dragon' or 'the fiendishly clever plan' in their own words.

Extension: In groups, they can record their presentations using a computer.

2. Dig deeper

Objective

To understand what they read.

What you need

Photocopiable page 47 'Comprehension check', copies of *How to Train Your Dragon*.

What to do

- A comprehension task with varied and graded questions helps to assess reading levels and can encourage higher-level thinking and problem-solving skills.

- Explain to the children that they are going to complete a reading task that will check their understanding of a text. Revise and, if necessary, explain the different types and levels of questions: closed questions (require simple 'yes' or 'no' responses); open questions (require details); multiple-choice questions (require you to choose an answer from ones provided); basic-level questions (require you to find the answer directly from the text); middle level questions (require you to analyse information or classify); higher-level questions (require you to interpret and apply the information – these can include visual literacy questions).

- Remind them that with a comprehension task, they should always begin by skimming and scanning the text for clues to what it is about (get the context), then read the text in detail, read through all the questions, then read the text again. Once they have followed these steps, they will be ready to begin! You can write these steps on the board for them to follow.

- Hand out photocopiable page 47 'Comprehension check' with the questions on Chapter 6. Read through the chapter and questions together. Give the children a reasonable time limit to complete the questions on their own.

Differentiation

Support: Go through each step with the children and read the text aloud.

3. Adventures

Objective

To draft and write.

What you need

Media resource 'A newsworthy event'.

What to do

- Open the media resource 'A newsworthy event' and read the news article. Ask the children to identify the main features. Guide the discussion and make a note of the correct terms on the board (headline, name of reporter, short paragraphs, columns, quotations, past tense).

- News articles also answer the questions Who? What? Where? When? Why? How? In groups, let the children find the answers to these questions.
  - Who is the article about? (the novices)
  - What happened to them? (banished)
  - Where did the event take place? (The Long Beach/Isle of Berk)
  - When did it happen? (Thor'sday Thursday)
  - Why did it happen? (They failed Initiation.)
  - How did the event occur? (They could not stop their dragons from fighting.)

- Ask the children to imagine they are reporters who were there when the Sea Dragon exploded. Brainstorm ideas for a heading (for example, Dragonius Explosionus, Giant Dragon Explodes, Blast on Berk, Sea Dragon Blasted to Pieces).

- Re-read Chapter 18. Make notes and find answers to the six questions. Let them plan a news article, write a draft and edit it carefully.

Differentiation

Support: Bring examples of news articles to school and go through them to identify the main features. Find answers to the six main questions.
Extension: Design the front page of a Viking newspaper. Include the name of the newspaper (for example, The Berk Times, The Viking Independent, The Barbaric Daily), a main article, other articles, pictures and adverts.

4. Meaning in context

Objective

To explain the meaning of words in context.

What you need

Printable page 'Mystery words', dictionaries, interactive activity 'Words in context'.

What to do

- Arrange the children into pairs. Give each pair a 'mystery word' from the words on printable page 'Mystery words'. Although the words may be familiar, the mystery lies in how to use them. Encourage the children to have at least one attempt at using the word in a sentence before looking it up. If they are stuck, let them use a dictionary to find the meaning of the word (or the root word) and the word class. Pairs should write a sentence then show you. When they've used the word correctly, they return the word and receive another word.

- Ask: *Is it easy or more difficult to understand a word on its own?* (more difficult) *What helps you find meaning in words?* (When we use the word with other words.)

- Use the mystery words to demonstrate how words connect in meaning when they are part of the same word family. Write the word 'wild' on the board. Invite the children to identify other words in this family: wildly, wilder, wilderness, wilds, wildest. Work another example. Give groups one mystery word to brainstorm related words. Bring the groups together and discuss their findings.

- Open the interactive activity 'Words in context' and let the children complete the activity, reinforcing words in context.

Differentiation

Support: Revise dictionary skills.
Extension: The children write their own sentences using the mystery words.

5. A Viking story

Objective

To create characters in narratives.

What you need

Copies of *How to Train Your Dragon*, interactive activity 'Create a cast'.

What to do

- Refer to the pictorial introduction of the main characters at the beginning of the book. Recap their names, characteristics and roles in the story.

- Arrange the children in small groups and assign one character per group. Display the following headings on the board: Name, Title, Role, Physical appearance, Special skills, Friends, Enemies, Dragon. Guide them to write a short profile for their character using these key headings. They can scan the book for ideas. Bring the groups together and have volunteers read each group's profile. Allow time for discussion and for groups to exchange ideas and incorporate suggestions into their profile.

- Ask the children to imagine getting the chance to give the author ideas for another story in the series. To be original, they must come up with a new cast. Using the interactive activity 'Create a cast', they should introduce four new characters, giving each one a Viking name with a brief profile showing the link between the name and the character. They should use the key headings on the board but fill in their own details. Assess originality and ability to match Viking names to characters.

Differentiation

Support: Make up profiles for characters from the story that are not included in the front of the book, such as Mogadon the Meathead, Thuggory the Meathead, Valhallarama, Old Wrinkly.

Extension: Print each profile onto A4 paper and include a picture of the character.

6. Listen up

Objective

To write from memory simple sentences, dictated by the teacher, that include words and punctuation taught so far.

What you need

Printable page 'Dictation station', individual whiteboards or paper, dictionaries.

What to do

- Practise auditory skills through various games. The children sit in groups of eight or ten. Choose someone to begin. The first person must begin by saying: 'I went into a cave and found…' and name one object. The next person repeats this phrase, including the first object, and must add another object to the list. Each person has a turn to add something to the list. The player who cannot repeat the list from the beginning, in the correct order, sits out! Continue until one person is left.

- In another auditory game, each child should have a whiteboard or paper to write on. Ask the children to write down any keyword from the story. Everyone should stand up. Give any of the following commands: 'Sit if…your word ends with "s"… your third letter is "r"… your word is a proper noun… your word rhymes with "work".' Continue until one person is standing.

- Explain that you will dictate sentences for the children to remember and write as accurately as possible. Use the graded sentences on printable page 'Dictation station' according to the appropriate level.

- The children should listen as you read a sentence twice then write the sentence in their workbooks. At the end, let them check their spelling and punctuation.

Differentiation

Support: Read only the sentences from section 1 from the printable page.

Extension: Include any sentences from sections 1–3 from the printable page.

Comprehension check

● Read Chapter 6 then answer the questions below.

1. What animal is described in this chapter? _____

2. List eight other sea creatures mentioned in the text. _____
   _____
   _____

3. How long had the creature been there? _____

4. What type of bed is a seabed? _____

5. What tells us that this animal is dangerous? _____
   _____

6. Find words in the text that mean the following:

   A bare, forsaken place _____

   A deep sleep or unconsciousness _____

   Very hungry _____

   Throat _____

7. What punctuation marks are used in the title?

   ☐ Capital letter   ☐ Ellipses

   ☐ Comma   ☐ All of the above

8. What figurative language is 'underwater mountain'?

   ☐ Simile   ☐ Alliteration

   ☐ Metaphor   ☐ Personification

9. Explain the purpose of this chapter. How does it fit into the rest of the story?
   _____
   _____
   _____

SCHOLASTIC

Available in this series:

978-1407-16066-5

978-1407-16053-5

978-1407-16054-2

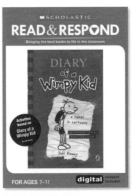

978-1407-16055-9

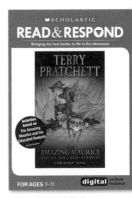

978-1407-16056-6

978-1407-16057-3

978-1407-16058-0

978-1407-16059-7

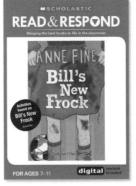

978-1407-16060-3

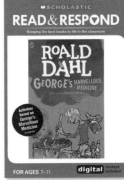

978-1407-16061-0

978-1407-16062-7

978-1407-16063-4

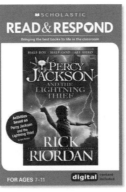

978-1407-16064-1

978-1407-16065-8

978-1407-16052-8

978-1407-16067-2

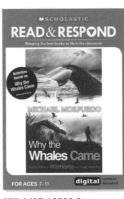

978-1407-16068-9

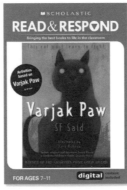

978-1407-16069-6

978-1407-16070-2

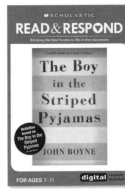

978-1407-16071-9

To find out more, call: 0845 6039091
or visit our website www.scholastic.co.uk/readandrespond